Introducing
Nonfiction Writing
In the Early Grades

Jodi Weisbart Mahoney

Lessons, Activities, and Graphic
Organizers That Teach Young Children
What Nonfiction Is and How to Write It

SCHOLASTIC
PROFESSIONAL BOOKS

NEW YORK ● TORONTO ● LONDON ● AUCKLA
MEXICO CITY ● NEW DELHI ● HONG KONG ● E

Dedication

*To the students, teachers, and families of P.S. 3 for giving me the space
to grow and spread my wings.*

Acknowledgments

Teaching is a collaborative effort. My teacher-heroes know how to
bounce ideas off of one another, consider each other's ideas and
incorporate them into their classrooms. I feel extremely lucky to be part
of such a learning community in both my school and my school district.
A heartfelt thanks to my staff developers Hindy List and Lucy Rubin for
allowing me to experiment with writing in my classroom and for delighting
in its success. Thank you to my student teacher Lauren Karp who blessed
our classroom for an entire year and worked tirelessly with me on this
curriculum. I also am indebted to my K/1 colleagues, who have been
endlessly supportive and interested in this work and who have shared their
success stories with me.

My editors, Wendy Murray, Joanna Davis-Swing, and Ray Coutu, have
all been wonderfully supportive of all of my writing. Thank you for
making writing books such a pleasant experience. And finally, thank you
to my friends and family who continue to buoy me with their interest, love,
and support in all of my endeavors. It is because of this support that I am
able to share my stories with others.

Front cover design by James Safarti
Interior design by Sarah Morrow
Cover and interior photographs by James Levin

ISBN: 0-439-33816-6
Copyright © 2002 by Jodi Weisbart Mahoney
Printed in USA

2 3 4 5 6 7 8 9 10   40   09 08 07 06 05 04 03

Contents

Foreword

"And what does the cow say?" we ask toddlers, and smile in delight as they answer, "Moo!" At the zoo, we grin as they hold out their 25-cents-worth-of-baby-lamb-and-goat pellets tentatively and get slobbered on. My daughter's first words are "Big Boy," our cat's name. She tosses little objects at Big Boy to see if he'll run from his food bowl. My two-year-old son presses his face against a glass jar to watch tiny transparent tadpoles fluttering their tails. "They be frogs like these?" he asks, pointing to the frog tank nearby. He looks back and forth carefully, doing animal research.

So when Jodi asked me last year if I thought the children in her K/l class were ready to do animal research, I said sure, knowing they'd probably already been doing it for years. What I didn't know then was how much was possible, how far they could go.

The project started with Jodi's belief in the children, in what they already knew, and what they were capable of finding out. The students created animal webs that reflected their knowledge and gave them the confidence to learn more. Jodi had them work on their webs in small groups, then with partners, and finally on their own. She supported them every step of the way, with mini-lessons on a variety of topics—from writing things down when you can't yet spell to finding information in a table of contents when you're just learning to read.

She modeled herself as a learner and went through all the steps with her class. She surrounded students with books. She created templates to help them organize their writing, and they, in turn, created more.

They learned how to share resources and ideas, how to revise and edit, how to publish, and how to make the animal-expert hats they wore proudly to their culminating celebration. They became a community of 22 focused readers and writers, 22 little engines who believed they could, and did, every day.

Introducing Nonfiction Writing in the Early Grades is a carefully conceived blueprint of how to do nonfiction writing with young children, in purposeful and fun ways. An invaluable resource, the book maps out a course of study for animal research, which can easily be adapted to fit any nonfiction topic. It is practical, thoughtful, and organized. And it reads like a conversation with a colleague down the hall. Most important, it shows how to develop independence and confidence in students. Indeed, with Jodi's fine book, even if your students aren't doing bird research, they all end up learning to fly.

Lucy Rubin
Literacy Staff Developer
Community School District 2, New York City

Introduction

Last year, when I visited Sharon Taberski's first-grade class at the Manhattan New School, the students' recent nonfiction publications about animals were on display. I remember looking through their work and being amazed by the level of detail and the depth of understanding the students were able to communicate. I was also amazed by Sharon's expectations of her students. I didn't think children so young could write nonfiction. But, clearly, she did.

Visiting Sharon's class made me think about my own experience writing nonfiction. When was I introduced to the genre? I clearly remembered doing my first research paper in the fifth grade. My classmates and I spent the entire year learning how to do research, use resources, and take notes. The result was a 30-page paper on one of the 13 colonies, which I wrote by hand since personal computers were just beginning to enter homes. I was thrilled and used my research skills from that day forward. I assumed that learning to do research, and writing nonfiction based on that research, was a fifth-grade rite of passage.

During my first year of teaching fourth and fifth graders, I tried to recreate that experience. I taught my students how to do research, using various resources, and how to organize information into an outline. I thought, based on my experience, that the early grades had given them a good foundation in fiction, and there was something almost magical about fifth grade. Something that would turn them into researchers who could write about facts, with just a nudge from me. And they did. They rose to the challenge and wrote well-documented, well-organized research papers.

Looking back, however, I realize my students were caught up in the mechanics of writing nonfiction—filling in note cards, collecting a bibliography, using footnotes. Although those were important parts of our research, I was overlooking other matters such as writing with expression and sharing expertise.

When I began teaching kindergarten and first grade, I found that young children, without having done formal research, were already experts on a variety of topics. They shared newly acquired information with me each day—often as they greeted me in the morning. Sometimes, they shared it in class discussions. And sometimes, they shared it just out of the blue, when I least expected it. My writing program included having students write about themselves, since they were, indeed, experts on that topic. However, when I realized that they were experts on other topics, too, I decided to build nonfiction writing into my program, hoping to tap the wealth of information my students held and open up new worlds for them.

To my delight, I found that nonfiction writing can and should be learned early. Young students, even kindergarteners, can handle nonfiction writing if they are given the right tools. This book chronicles my implementation of a nonfiction-writing study, and how that study dramatically changed the kinds of writing my young students produced.

Chapter 1

Unearthing Nonfiction for Young Writers

This chapter lays the foundation for introducing nonfiction writing in your classroom. I provide a rationale for my study and the steps and timeframe it took to complete it. From there, I discuss important issues such as finding the expert in every child, recruiting outside assistance, and helping students distinguish fiction from nonfiction.

Rationale for a Nonfiction Study

Before taking on nonfiction, my students wrote about a topic they knew well: themselves. At first, their writing was fresh. But after a few months, it began to lose its luster. I started feeling that my students needed something else. It was time to introduce a new genre. Moving from being experts on themselves to experts on other topics gave my students a chance to take their writing further.

I expected that writing nonfiction would be a challenge for my students, but one that would elevate their thinking—honor their knowledge and allow them to build upon it. So, to ease the transition from personal writing to nonfiction writing, I took a number of steps. I chose a topic that the children were interested in and could relate to: animals. I recruited family members to assist with research. Older relatives would help the children make sense of difficult concepts and language often found in nonfiction texts. I planned to help students research and organize their information. We would learn how to find information about animals in books. We would study published nonfiction texts, looking closely at their structures. And we would figure out how to communicate clearly our ideas to others.

This book chronicles our study of animals, but the concepts and procedures can be applied to any topic. For example, my colleague Sue Thomas used the structure for a worm study in her class. Another colleague, Ed Chang, used the templates described in Chapter 4 to help his students organize their thoughts for their friendship study.

Steps in a Nonfiction Study

A study typically takes place over eight weeks. In that time, we:

- choose a nonfiction topic: animals.
- use thematic webs to help capture what we already know about the topic.
- gather resources and use them to research the topic.
- revisit our webs and add newly acquired information.
- use templates to organize our writing into main ideas.
- compile our templates into chapters.
- compile our chapters into individual books about animals.
- share our knowledge through writing.

Each step is explored in depth in the following chapters.

A Week-by-Week Overview

Week 1:   Determining what nonfiction is
           Choosing a topic
           Modeling a web in groups and partners

Week 2:   Creating webs independently
           Gathering resources
           Using the index
           Using the table of contents
           Reading nonfiction texts

Week 3:   Reading nonfiction texts, continued
           Moving from creating webs to creating texts
           Creating templates

Weeks 4-6: Creating templates, continued
            Moving beyond one animal

Weeks 7-8: Writing a table of contents
            Writing an "About the Researcher" page
            Preparing for publishing

Week 8:   Celebrating published books as a class

Finding the Expert in Every Child

I believe that every child is an "expert" on something. On certain topics, children are the hosts of vast amounts of information. My job, then, is to hone in on what they know and help them realize where they are experts. This is easier for some students than for others—especially those who are eager to share all they know. Each morning, I am greeted with hellos, smiles, and, without fail, at least one piece of trivia, such as this one from Declan:

Declan: Jodi, did you know that Pterodactyls could fly?
Long necks were called Diplodocus, and
Triceratops had three horns?

Jodi: No, I don't know very much about dinosaurs,
but you sound like you know a lot about

9

them. Where did you learn so much about dinosaurs?

Declan: My dad and I were reading a book together last night.

With students who are not so verbal, I look for their areas of interests and then talk about them in informal conversations. Donna, for example, was particularly quiet. As she settled in one morning, I approached her.

Jodi: Donna, I was remembering this morning that you love animals.

Donna: Mmmm-hmmm.

Jodi: And I was remembering that you love to read animal stories and look at animal books.

Donna: (*Nods her head.*)

Jodi: So I was thinking that you must *really* know a lot about animals.

Donna: (*Shrugs.*)

Jodi: Is there one animal that you know a lot about?

Donna: Dogs.

Jodi: What do you know about dogs?

Donna: They're cute.

Jodi: What else do you know?

Donna: I have a dog. So I know what they like to do and what they like to eat. And what they do when they are mad.

Jodi: Wow, you know a lot about dogs. Today, maybe you could start writing down the things you already know. Then, we can start to look for new information.

Conversations like these build confidence in students who are uncertain about what they know and can do. Over time, students begin to realize that they are, indeed, experts on lots of topics, from outer space to animals, to how things work, to places in the city, and around the world. I find that information spills out of them when I ask good questions and give thoughtful responses. As soon as students learn it, they are eager to tell it. They are ready to share their knowledge through nonfiction writing.

Recruiting Outside Assistance

Before a study, I send a letter home to families explaining the involvement I will need. Since one of my goals is to enable students to share their knowledge and passion the best way they can, I encourage parents to work with their children in a variety of ways. Children might draw pictures, give dictation, create letter strings, write sentences with invented spelling, or write whole paragraphs of

> Dear Families,
>
> Our inquiry on animals is off and going! Your child is starting to organize what he/she knows and what he/she doesn't know yet.
>
> <u>For homework</u> (ongoing)
> 1.) As you read nonfiction books about animals together, choose one animal to focus on.
> 2.) Then, help your child make a web (example below) based on information you are learning.
>
> *where sharks live* · ocean — **Sharks** — *what sharks eat* -fish eat · *what sharks look like* · sharp teeth · fins
>
> 3.) You may want to make one web that includes the following things:
> – what the animal eats   – how it moves
> – where it lives   – how it gets its
> – how it protects itself   food
> – how it cares for its babies
> – what it looks like
> 4.) Please make sure that your child is an <u>active</u> participant in this process and understands the web you make together. He/she will be using it to write nonfiction animal books.
> *Thanks —
> Jodi*

Letter to families

information. I also ask parents to help their children find books on their topics, sift through those books together, and organize information they find into webs.

Parents volunteer in my classroom as well. They help students find information about their topic in books, read difficult captions and texts to them, and add new information to their webs. We use one another, along with my student teacher, as resources.

In conjunction with in-class helpers, I also tap our librarian. During library period, the children look for texts on their topics with the librarian's guidance. In the process, the children pick up valuable skills for locating books they need. If there were no library in my school, trips to the public library would be part of my study. It is important for students to get not only a sense of what resources are available, but where those resources can be found.

Helping Students Distinguish Nonfiction From Fiction

Comparing fiction and nonfiction is a key introductory component to the study. My students tend to come with basic knowledge on the difference between fiction books and nonfiction books (i.e., that one is made up and the other is true.) My goals, then, are to "unearth" nonfiction texts for my students—to introduce the genre and make them comfortable with its format and function. I eventually have them write nonfiction works of their own.

I start by helping students understand that nonfiction books' primary purposes are to share information and build knowledge. I do this by comparing nonfiction texts with something more familiar: fiction texts. It's important to note that this comparison is not a full-blown study of its own. It creeps into our work as a frequent topic of whole-class discussions. That way, over time, students learn both obvious and subtle differences between the genres.

I introduce the concept in a whole-class meeting. I ask if anyone knows what "fiction" or "nonfiction" means. Students usually offer a few ideas, such as "true stories" or "imaginary stories," but aren't sure to which genres the terms apply. So I give them working definitions:

- Fiction is not true. It's based on stories that are mostly made up.

- Nonfiction is true. It's based on facts, things that we know are true.

For the next few weeks, as I read an animal story to the students each morning, I ask them, "Is this fiction or nonfiction? Is it made up or true?" This enhances our study, as students continually gain experience identifying different types of texts.

Sometimes students have a hard time making this distinction, especially when the book contains realistic events and feelings, such as *Verdi* by Janell Cannon:

Jodi:	So, what do you think about *Verdi*? Is it fiction or nonfiction?
Noah:	It is about a snake, so that part is true.
Jodi:	So do you think this is nonfiction?
Amanda:	No, the snake talks to his friends.

Snakes don't talk.

Jodi: So what do you think it is then?

Amanda: Fiction.

Elijah: Well it's a little bit true and a little bit non-true.

Jodi: Sometimes fiction books have some things that are inspired by real feelings or events in life—but they are mostly untrue, so they are still fiction.

Elijah: Then this is fiction.

To reinforce students' understanding of the distinction between fiction and nonfiction, I have them use reading logs to keep track of the genres they're reading. In *On Solid Ground*, Sharon Taberski details how her students color code book titles according to genre. Inspired by that system, I have students color code books in both their in-school and at-home reading logs—blue for nonfiction, red for fiction, and yellow for poetry. Later in our study, as we move beyond books and into periodicals, students add another color to our reading logs: green for magazines, which adds depth. This small requirement encourages students to think about the distinction between fiction and nonfiction regularly. Again, we don't harp on that distinction; it merely becomes a part of our understanding of what we are reading.

In addition to noting differences between fiction and nonfiction

---

Name _____
Date _____

READING LOG
Please record titles of books you read each day!

MONDAY   1. _____ ☐
           2. _____ ☐
           3. _____ ☐

TUESDAY   1. _____ ☐
           2. _____ ☐
           3. _____ ☐

WEDNESDAY 1. _____ ☐
           2. _____ ☐
           3. _____ ☐

THURSDAY 1. _____ ☐
           2. _____ ☐
           3. _____ ☐

FRIDAY   1. _____ ☐
           2. _____ ☐
           3. _____ ☐

Please color boxes as
Blue=Nonfiction Red=Fiction
Yellow=Poetry

Color-coded reading log

during reading workshop, we delve into reading strategies, focusing on ways to approach and comprehend nonfiction works. (See Chapter 3 for details.)

This chapter focused on laying the foundation for a nonfiction study. The next chapter details how I use that foundation to introduce the web as organizational tool—a tool we rely on to be successful.

Professional Books

A Matter of Fact: Using Factual Texts in the Classroom by Pamela Green (Portage & Main Press)

On Solid Ground: Strategies for Teaching Reading K-3 by Sharon Taberski (Heinemann)

Chapter 2

Planning With Webs

 In response to our classroom work and homework described in Chapter 1, my students choose an animal that interests them. Generally, they are eager to start writing, but they are not at all interested in planning. Planning is crucial, though, because it helps them determine what they have to say. My job, therefore, is to convey that importance. In my first mini-lesson, I introduce a planning web that helps students access what they know about their topic, identify gaps in their understanding, and incorporate new information as they gather it.

Introducing a Web

Simply stated, a web is a visual organizer of information. The main idea goes in the center, with details related to that idea surrounding it. If relationships among details are identified, they can be linked with lines and labels.

Before I model how to create a web, I choose my own animal to research, one that none of the children have chosen: a monkey. I plan to use the monkey throughout the study, in my mini-lessons.

With the children gathered around me, I begin.

Jodi: Today we are going to start working on our animal books. Most of you have already chosen an animal to research. The animal I've chosen is the monkey. I already know some things about monkeys from reading books and seeing them at the zoo. You probably know some things about monkeys, too. What kinds of things do you know?

Anthony: They swing.

Declan: They have fur.

Isa: They are mammals.

Sierra: They live in trees.

Jodi: Let's get those ideas down on paper. Before I start writing my book about monkeys, it's important that I write down all the things I already know. I'm going to use a web to help me organize my information. That way, I'll be able to see what I need to find out more about. I can use beginning sounds, words, or pictures to add information to our web.

I begin making my web on chart paper, which I will revisit later. In a circle at the center of the chart, I write "monkey."

Jodi: What do we know about monkeys?

Shawnee: Monkeys have brown fur.

Jodi: So this is what a monkey looks like. I'll write "brown and furry" on my web. What else do we know about monkeys?

Declan: They eat bananas.

Jodi:	Oh, so that's different than what they look like. That's what they eat. I'll put that on a different part of my web. What could I do if I didn't know how to write the word *bananas*? Should I just forget about that?
Amanda:	No. You could draw a picture.
Jodi:	Good idea. I'll draw a picture.

I continue stretching out words and using pictures as ways of getting information on the web. From there, I introduce the idea of grouping related details together by placing all of the information on eating in the same place. The children may or may not apply this level of organization in their webs, which is fine. My goal for now is introducing them to the concept.

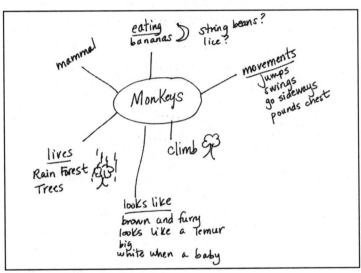

Jodi's whole-class web: stage 1

Working in Small Groups

When introducing a new skill, concept, or genre, I always have students work in small groups, then pairs, and then on their own. I find that this gradual movement toward independence fosters a willingness to take risks in writing because students have the support they need early on. Therefore, as part of the nonfiction study, I ask students to try making webs in writing groups. I assign each group an animal and ask members to make a web containing all of the things they know about that animal.

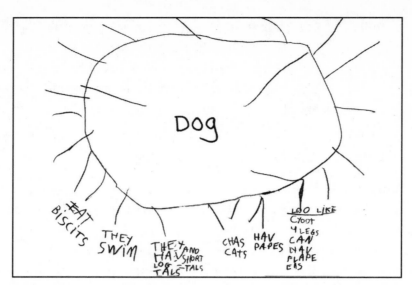

Students in the dog group write what they know in their web and begin to organize some of their information into a category "Looks Like." They record a good amount of information about dogs:

- Eat biscuits
- They swim
- They have long tails and short tails
- Chase cats

- Have puppies
- Looks Like: cute, 4 legs, can have floppy ears

The snake group uses pictures and words to share their knowledge. Here are the ideas members record:

- They are 10 feet long
- It rattles
- It camouflages
- It sheds skin
- They eat rats

- It lives in the desert
- It slithers
- They lay eggs
- Some are poison

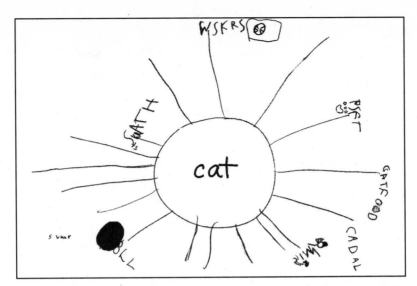

The cat group works extremely hard on getting their ideas down. Members sound out words and use some pictures to support their ideas. This is what they know about cats:

- Whiskers
- Scratches
- Balls
- Paws for feet
- Cat food
- Cuddle
- Wise

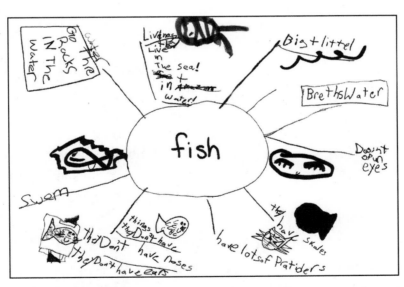

Students in the fish group use pictures and text as well. However, their pictures do not support their text as strongly. Their writing is fluent enough that it stands alone, without supporting pictures. Also evident is the beginning of an organizational structure. Students have begun to create categories, "Things they don't have" and "Living." They know that fish:

- Go through rocks in the water
- Live in the sea and in water
- Are big and little
- Breathe water
- Don't open eyes
- Have scales
- Have lots of predators
- Don't have noses or ears
- Swim

Understanding Fact Versus Opinion

The animal study opens many doors of exploration for us. For example, when webs contain statements such as "dogs are cute," it provides the perfect opening to discuss the difference between fact and opinion.

Jodi: You guys have a lot of great information on these webs. I see some things that are facts and some things that are your opinions. For example, on the dog group's web, it says dogs have four legs. Do we all agree that dogs have four legs?

Class: Yes.

Jodi: Then it says, "Dogs are cute." Does everyone agree that dogs are cute?

Class: Yes.

Jodi: You all think that every single dog is cute? There isn't one person who doesn't think that dogs are cute?

Class: (*Mumbles.*)

Jodi: It may be your opinion that dogs are cute, but that isn't a fact. A fact is something we *all* agree is true. Authors include many facts in nonfiction writing, and try not to include their opinions. So, let's look at another example. On the snake group's web, it says, "it sheds skin." Is that a fact or an opinion?

Cosmo: Fact.

Jodi: How do you know?

Cosmo: Because all snakes shed skin.

Jodi: How about if it said, "snakes are slimy?"

Sierra: That's an opinion. That's what you think. Not everybody might think that they are slimy.

Jodi: Great. So when we are working on our nonfiction writing, let's be careful to try to keep our opinions about animals separate from the facts.

Creating Webs Independently

Once students explore webs in groups and with partners, they are ready to try creating them on their own. Since there are children at every stage of writing development in my classroom, I expect some will be able to write detailed webs. Some will use pictures and words to depict what they know. And some will need help getting any information down at all. I plan to meet with those students first.

Esmir

As the rest of the class gets settled in their writing groups, I go over to Esmir, who is studying cheetahs. He will need support understanding the organizational structure to get started. I notice that he has brought in a few pages of printed information from the Internet.

Jodi: Esmir, it looks like you have a lot of information here. What can you tell me about cheetahs? (I write "cheetah" on his paper to get him started and give him the correct spelling for "cheetah," a word he will be using frequently.)

Esmir: A cheetah bites.

Jodi: Let's write that on your web. Where can you find the word "cheetah?"

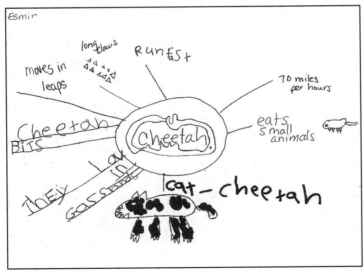

Esmir's cheetah web

Esmir points to the word cheetah and uses it for reference as he writes it on a line from the center ring. Then together we sound out "bites." He writes it next to where he has written cheetah.

Jodi: What else?

Esmir: Cheetahs have long claws.

Jodi: Can your write that or draw a picture that would show that?

Esmir draws 10 triangles depicting claws. I write the words "long claws" next to his picture.

For the next few minutes, Esmir and I continue to work on his web, taking turns writing. He uses pictures to illustrate the words I write for him. This collaborative effort solidifies the knowledge Esmir already has and gives him the confidence he needs to work on his web independently and eventually write his book.

Bryan

I work in a similar manner with Bryan, who has a lot of information on turtles but finds it difficult to sound out all of the words he wants to write. Bryan knows what he needs to do; he's just not sure how to do it. So over the next few days, we will add to his web together as he acquires more information about turtles. By focusing on the content of Bryan's web, it enables me to focus on the strategies he is using, too. For example, I notice that he is beginning to

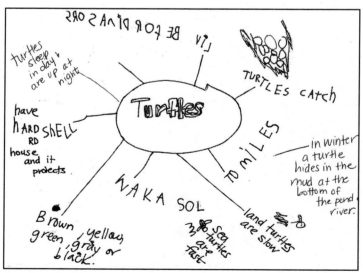

Bryan's turtle web

write a phrase backwards. I question him about it, and he writes the next phrase in the correct direction.

Cosmo

Next, I visit with Cosmo, an extremely independent writer, who is working on kangaroos. Cosmo's page is covered with writing. He has begun to organize his web in the same way I organized mine.

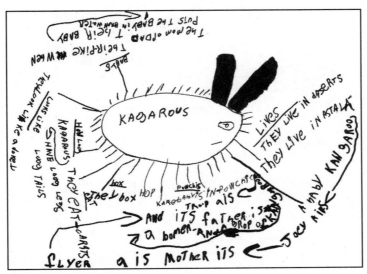

Cosmo's kangaroo web

Cosmo is working well by himself, so our conference winds up being more of a "check-in."

Isa

I confer with Isa that day as well and am fascinated by her web, which is filled with "Did you know?" statements. Already her voice is coming through. It is clear that Isa has read many nonfiction texts and, as such, is familiar with questioning as a method of sharing knowledge. I admire how it has crept into her writing. I plan to share this method later in the unit.

Isa's tiger web

Beginning the Research Process

We visit and revisit our webs often throughout the study. In essence, they become our working drafts. The next day, at the beginning of writer's workshop, I ask the children where I could find out more information about my animal, the monkey. They suggest books and magazines around our room. We find a book about monkeys. I skim the table of contents (knowing that I would formally introduce using a table of contents later) and find a section on what monkeys eat. I turn to that page and read it to the students. We learn that monkeys eat insects, plants, and birds' eggs. They are hunters during the day.

Jodi: Hmmm…we learned some new information there. Where do you think we can put that information so that we won't forget about it?

Eli: On our web.

Jodi: That's a good idea. Anywhere on our web?

Eli: No, where we wrote about what it eats.

Jodi: Ah, so let's add our new information to our web.

I add the information to my web, hoping that the children begin to see this exercise as an essential part of writing. I then ask students to work in pairs for that day's writing workshop, on webs for their own animal or their partner's.

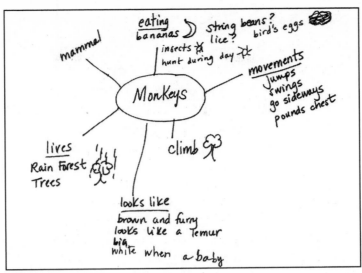

Jodi's whole-class web: stage 2

On the following day, I find a book with a clear definition of "mammal" and, as a class, we return to my web.

Jodi: We have on our web that a monkey is a mammal. What does that mean?

Rachel: It gives its babies its milk?

Isa: Its babies are born from their tummies, not from eggs.

Jodi: Those are some ideas I had, too. I found a place in the book that describes what a mammal is. (*I read the definition and it mentions both of those ideas.*) Should we add that to our web?

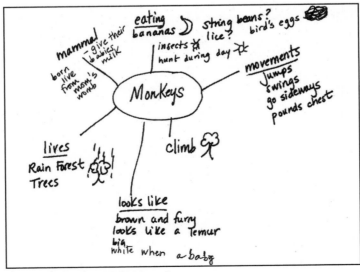

Jodi's whole-class web: stage 3

Class:	Yes.
Jodi:	Every day we gather more information about our animals and add to our web. Our web will help us plan our writing and share clearly all of the facts you know about your animals. As your continue to learn about your animals, you, too, will add to your webs.

Determining What to Research

Students often find it difficult to isolate gaps in their information. Conferring with them helps. I try to question students about the information they have and information they might need. I always begin by asking the student to share what he or she knows.

Jodi:	Anthony, what animal are you working on?
Anthony:	Alligators.
Jodi:	What do you know about alligators?
Anthony:	They have sharp teeth.
Jodi:	Let's write that on your web. What else?
Anthony:	Strong jaws.
Jodi:	Anthony, you already have some ideas about alligators. Let's keep writing down what you know and then we'll go look for some more information. Do you know where they live?
Anthony:	In swamps.
Jodi:	Do you know what they eat?
Anthony:	I think they eat beavers.
Jodi:	Really? Beavers?
Anthony:	Yes. I think so.
Jodi:	I'll write that down and when we look for information, we'll check it out because I'm not sure what they eat. Do you know how they take care of their babies?
Anthony:	No.
Jodi:	So now we are ready to go find some books on alligators.

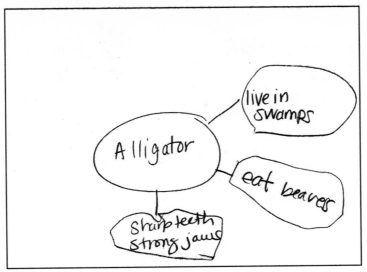

Anthony's alligator web

Creating Webs With Family Members

Students gather information at home, too, and work together with family members to create a separate web on their animals. By doing this, children make the information their own. I find it makes them more eager to write. With the family web, I can easily guide students during writing workshop, picking up where they left off with their families and helping them apply information to their class web. However, some children use their family webs *instead* of their class webs. Others go back and forth between webs, making sure they include all of the information they gather both at home and in school.

Declan's at-home learning experience was particularly rich. He:

- read books with his family, scouring them for phrases to add to his web.

- organized his information into categories, with the help of adult family members.

- wrote about his information.

By the time Declan arrived at school the next day, he knew so much about vultures he didn't need his web to write. However, I did. The web was a good source of information as I continued to help him write.

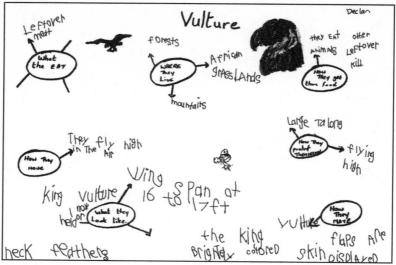

Declan's vulture web

Emma, a kindergartener, was not yet writing independently. Her mom, therefore, helped her make a web by writing down the information they had discovered together. When Emma came to school the next day, I spoke to her about her research. Although Emma could not read her web, she could tell me about things on it. Therefore, the web enabled me to understand what she knew and help her share that information in writing.

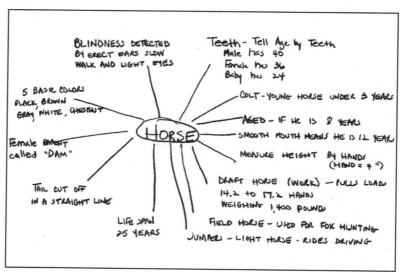

Emma's horse web

If a child's family doesn't have the time or resources to work on webs, either a student teacher or I work one-on-one with that child in class. We don't do this during writing workshop, however, since I want students to be writing about information during writing work-shop, not necessarily gathering it on a web. Finding one-on-one time is not always easy. I sometimes work with students during work centers, or pull them out of a special such as gym, computer, or library time. Sometimes I have a student teacher work with them during morning meeting. Whenever we can carve out time, we work with these students.

At this point, the students are getting used to using the web as an organizational device. The next step is to give them tools that can help them find the answers to their questions and provide new information. Introducing them to those tools is tricky. The next chapter takes a closer look at that process.

Chapter 3

Finding and Using Research Tools

Students generally know some things about animals from life experience. But life experience isn't always the best source of information for nonfiction writing. We need to give students tools for doing research, such as books, magazines, and encyclopedias, and demonstrate how to use them. In this chapter, I demonstrate how I help students find resources, use an index and table of contents, and apply reading strategies to nonfiction texts.

Because using resources can be complicated for young students, it's important to introduce them gradually and with a great deal of support. Also, exploring them should be a team effort between teacher and student, family and student, and student and student.

Gathering Resources

My students do a good deal of research inside and outside the classroom. So, for the animal study, they take books out of the local library and bring them to school. I make available lots of resources on animals, which I gather from our school and classroom libraries. I ask students to bring in magazines such as *Your Big Backyard* and *Ranger Rick*. These wonderful magazines are written for emergent and transitional readers. They have incredible pictures, fun facts, and loads of information. Magazines for adults, such as *National Geographic* and *Scientific American*, require assistance for research, but are helpful nonetheless, especially for their beautiful photographs.

Over time, our classroom library becomes more specialized. We have animal periodicals, nonfiction texts on single animals, and anthologies on many different kinds of animals. Because I spend a lot of time modeling how to use these resources, my students become expert librarians. If they come across information that would be useful to a classmate while doing their own research, I encourage them to share that information. As a result, my students become one another's best resources.

> ### Favorite Periodicals for an Animal Study
>
> *Discover*
> *Muse*
> *National Geographic*
> *Ranger Rick*
> *Your Big Backyard*

Using the Index

Even though we are early into the research process, the children are familiar with the animals they've chosen. They've gathered information about them on their webs. Most, if not all, of them know how to spell or at least read their animal's name. Knowledge like this helps as we work on using text features, such as the index and the table of contents.

In my first mini-lesson on research tools, I introduce students to using the index. I post my monkey web on the easel, making the point that we are going to continue gathering information from books to add to our webs. Therefore, it's important that our webs are accessible.

I start by asking students how to find books with information on monkeys. They suggest looking in our basket of animal books. I check the basket and find only one book on monkeys—a book from which we've already gathered information. We decide we need other books. I pull out a stack of animal anthologies, which I had assembled earlier, and show them to the class.

Jodi: These books are about lots of animals. How can we find out if there is information in here about monkeys?

Noah: You could look at the pictures inside.

Jodi: That's a great idea, Noah! I could quickly look through the pages and, if I see a monkey, I'll know that there is some information in here for my project. That's one good way. Any other ideas? (*No one has any.*) Another way is to use the index. The index is a list of all of the animals in the book and the pages they appear on. The index is always in the back of the book and is in alphabetical order. So let's see, "monkey" starts with the letter…

Class: M!

Jodi: (*Opens to the index and finds "M" with finger.*) And how do I spell the rest of *monkey*? Can you look on our web?

Class: -o-n-k-e-y

Jodi: So I'm going to look in the M section for that word. Here it is…*monkey*, pages 53 and 54. So now I'll start with page 53 (*Flips to the page*) …and here it is: information on monkeys. The index is a great way to find information on your animals. Today, if you are looking for more information to add to your webs, try using the index or looking through the pictures in books. (*Looks for new information on pages 53 and 54, scans the pictures, captions, and subtitles.*) It says here that monkeys eat insects. Let's add that to our web. Where should we add it?

Bryan: Where it says what it eats.

Jodi: Okay, under where I've written "bananas," I'll write insects. I can even copy the word "insects" from the book, so I'll know just how to spell it. (*Adds the word to the web.*)

My students, like students in most classrooms, are at every stage of reading development. Therefore, in my mini-lessons, I encourage all kinds of strategies, to give every child a way to find information. The same is true for writing. Some students use pictures to depict their ideas. Some write words. Some tell me information that I transcribe because they do not yet have the tools to write it themselves. As a rule of thumb, I honor students' knowledge and help them share it with others in the best way they can.

Using the Table of Contents

In a mini-lesson, I tell students that the table of contents offers a new way to read books. You may decide to read only parts of a book, parts that contain specific information. You don't need to read the entire book from cover to cover.

I demonstrate this using a nonfiction big book, which I also use in shared reading for the week to work on strategies for making sense of nonfiction texts. In this way, students simultaneously work on comprehension and research skills.

Jodi: Yesterday, we talked about using the index to help us find out if the book has information on our animal. Today, we'll look at the table of contents. The table of contents is found in the front of the book. Where was the index?

Declan: In the back.

Jodi: The table of contents lists what's inside this book and where to find it. It is similar to the index in that way. This book is about spiders. Let's look at the table of contents and see what kind of information is in this book. (We read the contents together.) What page would we turn to for information on spiders' webs?

Rachel: 8.

Jodi: What page would we turn to for information on what a spider looks like?

Lucian: Maybe page 2.

Jodi: How did you know that, Lucian?

Lucian: It says "The Spider's Body" so that will maybe tell us what the body looks like.

As a class we continue to move back and forth between the table of contents and the text. The children begin to see how to read this text for information, with the help of the table of contents and index. Already they are becoming independent researchers.

Strategies for Reading Nonfiction Texts

Beyond locating information in books, students also need strategies for making sense of that information. Reading nonfiction texts is different from reading fiction texts. When reading fiction, we carry the story in our heads, relating to the characters, making connections to ourselves and the world around us. When reading a nonfiction text, we generally read for information. We don't necessarily need to carry all the previous information to understand the new information.

Unlike in fiction, there are often graphics in nonfiction, such as photographs and illustrations, that support the text and help our understanding. It is these subtle differences that I introduce to my students. I want them to be able to move through a text, seek information, and move beyond a passage that is difficult to comprehend. Teaching them strategies like these enables them to take risks in reading and research. I believe that, by giving them these tools, I am opening the doors to nonfiction.

Each day, through our shared reading, we discuss new strategies for reading nonfiction. (See chart on page 35.) We also talk about them during writing share, when students typically exchange ideas for finding information to add to their texts.

Ready for Research

At this point, the students are feeling empowered. They are eager researchers who enjoy scouring texts for information on their animals. But it's a fragile enthusiasm. In the upper grades, teachers sometimes bog down students by putting too much emphasis on citing sources. And that would definitely be the case here. I don't worry about it because my young writers know that the information they are gathering is not their own. In our conversations about fact and opinion, fiction and nonfiction, we talk about "what is true." The children see themselves as reporters of information. They know they've gotten their information from outside sources. At this point in their nonfiction writing development, that is good enough for me.

As we learn about various tools for research, we revisit our webs,

Ways to Comprehend Nonfiction Texts

1. Use pictures to access information from the text.
2. Use captions, labels, and titles for clues.
3. Skip hard words and come back to them.
4. Look for small words inside big words.
5. Use what you know and associations you have to help you figure out what the text might say.
6. Move around a page. (For example, read a caption, then a paragraph, then look at a photograph.)
7. Skip around a text for specific kinds of information. (For example, read for what animals eat or where they live.)
8. Skip a word, yet still understand the gist of the text. Don't get stuck on a scientific word or complicated name.

adding facts and details, and editing incorrect statements. I model this through mini-lessons, using my monkey web. We continue to look for categories about animals—what they eat, where they live, what they look like, how they protect themselves, and how they take care of their young. Some students' webs begin to reflect these categories, while others' remain random. The students use words, phrases, and pictures to represent information.

My class has spent a good deal of time working on our webs and revisiting them. We have skimmed books, scoured indexes, leafed through magazines, and used tables of contents. We know a lot about our animals (or at least we think we do) and we are ready to write. The next chapter shows how we move from researching to writing about our research.

Chapter 4

Writing About Our Research

The students have been working on their webs for about a week and have amassed a lot of information. They knew a lot to begin with—but not as much as they thought they did. They are now bursting with information and ready to begin writing.

In this chapter, I demonstrate how we use templates as organizers for writing. Eventually, students will compile these templates into individual books about animals. Some students will write about just one animal. Others will write about more than one, creating nonfiction anthologies, with each chapter focusing on a different animal.

The Value of Using Templates

I rarely give students a specific topic on which to write, or a way to write about it. Generally, they hold true artistic license. However, during a nonfiction study, I make an exception because I know students will benefit from clear, simple supports.

When students begin to write, I give them guidelines, suggestions, and organizational tools such as templates. My rationale is simple. I want students to be able to organize their writing, revisit parts of it, and add information as they learn. Templates help them do that. Without them, I fear students' writing would be a jumble of assorted facts, with little room for revising or editing. Templates help to move their writing forward.

Each template captures an information category that students focus on in their research. To create templates, I type out each category on a separate piece of paper:

1. What a _____ looks like

2. What a _____ eats

3. How a _____ moves

4. How a _____ grows

5. Where a _____ lives

6. How a _____ protects itself

7. How a _____ takes care of its babies

My hope is that students will see that templates help them organize their thoughts and communicate their ideas clearly to their readers. In time, many students create their own templates, on new categories they identify, as they write their books.

Introducing Templates

I show students the templates and point out the blank line on each one. Together, we determine that it makes sense to put an animal's name on each line. Using my web as a reference, I fill in the word "monkey" on my templates. Then, with my web and "What a monkey looks like" template, I model how to use information from my web to start writing.

Jodi:	On the web we created together there is information about what a monkey looks like. What does our web tell us?
Donna:	They are brown and furry.
Jodi:	Okay, so let's write that on our page about what a monkey looks like. What should we say?
Donna:	Monkeys are brown and furry.
Jodi:	"Monkeys," how do we spell that?
Declan:	Look at the web, m-o-n-k-e-y-s
Jodi:	Thank you. "Monkeys are..." we know "are." That's a word-wall word.
Class:	a-r-e
Jodi:	Monkeys are brown and furry. "Brown and furry." We've already figured out how to spell that on our web. So we'll refer to our web for the spelling.

What a **Monkey** looks like

Monkeys are brown and furry.

The class's first template based on information from Jodi's web

After writing the sentence about what monkeys look like, I move on to another template, even though my web contains more information on that subject. I want children to know that they do not have to "finish" one template before moving on to another. I expect their work to be fluid. I expect them to move back and forth between web, template, and resources.

Create a Writers' Word Wall

The word wall is an effective resource for the writers in my classroom. It starts out as a blank bulletin board, labeled with upper- and lowercase letters. Throughout the year, during our writing mini-lessons, we add words to the word wall that we use frequently as writers. Often words come from our weekly poems. Together, we discuss why a word is appropriate for the wall. We also discuss under which letter the word should go, giving us an opportunity to explore the word's initial sound.

Jodi: What's next? Ah, "What a monkey eats." Does our web tell us anything about what monkeys eat?

Justin: They eat insects and plants and birds' eggs. (*Justin uses both the pictures and text on my web to help him read the information.*)

Jodi: So let's write, "A monkey eats insects and plants and birds' eggs."

What a **Monkey** eats

A monkey eats insects and plants and birds' eggs. Baby monkeys drink their mother's milk.

The class's second template

Again, I model how to refer to the web for spelling and use the template to form complete sentences. Then I send students off to work on a template of their choice during writers' workshop.

Using Templates Independently

For the next few weeks, children work on templates for their chosen animal. In the process, they may realize that they need more information. For example, Justin realizes that he doesn't know how snakes take care of their babies. Sierra doesn't have any idea how a panda grows. The templates and their webs often reveal information that's missing. When that happens, students go back to the books, apply new information to their webs, and then add it to their templates.

Some students work quickly. When they finish the templates for one animal, they begin the process again, on a different animal. Others work slowly, taking awhile to draw their pictures or write their words down. Again, I do not mind taking dictation, because it allows them to progress through the study at a reasonable pace. In most instances, these students have the knowledge, but, because of their stage of development, they are unable to write independently. That's where I can help.

As students are getting comfortable using templates, I keep my mini-lessons short and predictable. Each day, we fill in a new monkey template together, using my web as source of information.

How a **Monkey** moves

Monkeys climb trees.

How a **Monkey** grows

Monkeys come from their mom.

Where a **Monkey** lives

Monkeys live in trees.

More templates created by the class

When we get to the template "How a monkey protects itself," we run into a problem: There is no information on my web that tells us.

Jodi: So, how does a monkey protect itself? Is there anything on our web that gives us that information?

Noah: We don't know.

Jodi: What should we do? Should we skip it?

Liana: You could look it up in a book.

Jodi: That's a good idea. I could do some research today during writing workshop. If you come to a place that requires more research, you may not do much writing. That's okay. Some days you'll do more researching than writing. And other days you'll do lots of writing. While you work today, I'll try to find out how monkeys protect themselves.

The Look and Feel of a Researcher's Writing Workshop

At this stage, there's a buzz about the room. Children are sprawled out, on tables and on the floor, with their writing folders, books, magazines, and sticky notes in front of them. Some students are writing. Others are reading for information. Others are sharing their information with their peers. This writing workshop feels different from our usual quiet, more reflective time. And yet, it feels good. It feels productive. The students are working hard. Everyone is engaged and eagerly finding more about their topic.

Usually my students stay seated at tables during writing workshop, unless they are looking for a word around the room. If help is needed, it goes to them. However, for this study, students move more than usual since they are information seekers. There is purposeful and fluid movement throughout the workshop.

As such, at times the room feels chaotic, which makes me nervous. Maybe it's time to flash the lights, remind the children to lower the voices. I hold myself back from those impulses, though, because quiet is not what is needed. The buzz is appropriate for the work students are doing. It is the noise of knowledge being shared from book to student and from student to student. This different shape of a writing workshop intrigues me.

Conferring With Students

I move from student to student, conferring with them about their writing. Each student presents a different need. My role is to determine that need and help them address it. I do that largely through the questions I ask: How's it going? Where are you stuck? How can I help? Can you read me what you have already? Do we need to get more information? How and where can we find more information?

Alicia

I move to Alicia who is sitting ready to write at her table. She has the template "What a _____ looks like" and her butterfly web in front of her.

Alicia: I don't know what to write.

Jodi: Well, let's look at your web. You have lots of information on it already. Let's use that to help us write about butterflies. This template is for what a butterfly looks like. Let's fill in the word "butterfly" first.

Alicia: (*Fills in the word and looks back at me blankly.*)

Jodi: What do you know about what a butterfly looks like? On your web you wrote they have wings and antennae and are lots of colors.

Alicia: (*Nods her head.*)

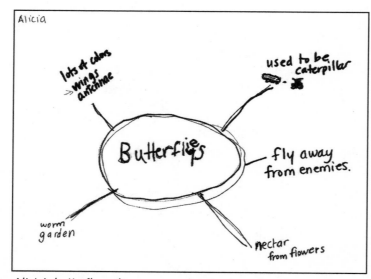

Alicia's butterfly web

Jodi: Could you write about that?

Alicia: (*Nods her head.*)

Jodi: I'll help you start ….Butterflies have wings. They have…

Alicia: Antennae.

Jodi: Keep going…you are on your way.

Alicia continues, finding it easy to apply her web text to her book text. However, when she gets to the page "How a butterfly grows," she feels overwhelmed by the concept of metamorphosis. Although Alicia could explain it orally, understandably she did not feel confident to convey her understanding in writing. Therefore, I take dictation. By writing down her words, I respect her understanding of the process and allow her to move on with the other pages for her book.

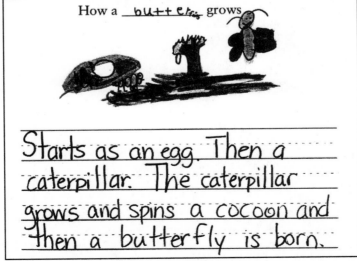

Alicia's templates, based on information from her web

Sierra

Sierra uses language, as well as information, from texts she reads in her web and writing. As Sierra read, she wrote down ideas about gorillas on her web. She then uses those ideas in her writing.

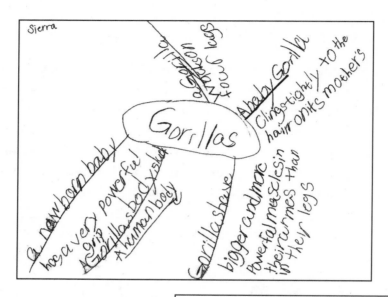

Sierra's gorilla web and templates

How a _Gorilla_ moves

A Gorilla wacks on four legs

A Gorilla shave bigger and more powerful muscles in ther arms

A newborn baby has a very powerful grip

Donna

Donna's web serves as a foundation of information for me. From it I can easily assess what she already knew about horses. I can then direct her to the template to begin working on.

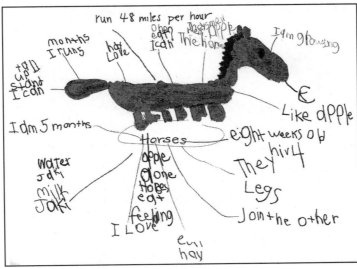

Donna's horse web

Donna also uses information in her book that does not appear on her web. From a book on horses, she found facts on the horse's anatomy. She was particularly fascinated by how quickly horses grow and change. She decided to use that information on her page "How a horse grows." Here her pictures, more than her words, suggest her understanding of what she read.

How a __HORSes__ grows

a Horses grows
one week old
Two week old three
week old four five
week week
old old

Donna's template

Liana

Sometimes we cannot find any information at all on a topic. For example, Liana couldn't find information on "How a ferret protects itself." When this happens, I encourage students to skip the page and publish their books without the information. This allows them to keep moving through the writing process, without getting bogged down in fact finding.

Generating Their Own Templates

Often students find information that does not fall into any of our predetermined template categories. For example, Cosmo wanted to include the fact that kangaroos are mammals in his book. Therefore, he created a page using a blank template that I provided.

What Kide of Mamels

KA39AR00s ARe MAMels.

Cosmo's self-generated kangaroo template:
"Kangaroos are mammals."

Making blank templates available allows students to broaden their focus. Some students stick to the templates I provide, but others go on to create their own, once they feel at ease with the organization and process. For example, Noah is researching and writing about cows. He feels it is crucial to share his understanding that cows are milk providers. So he writes, "They give us milk." I am thrilled that he feels free to move beyond the templates that I provide. (I hoped they would merely be a starting point.) Noah and I discuss what the heading should be and decide on "What do cows give us?" (See Appendix B for a reproducible template.)

What do ___CAOW___ give us?
                 cow

Noah's self-generated cow template: "They give us milk."

Moving Beyond One Animal: Creating Anthologies

Over time, I see students' template sets more as chapters within a larger book, rather than books unto themselves. So I encourage students to create animal anthologies, made up of information on more than one animal. Many of our research resources had information on more than one animal, after all. If the authors of those books could structure their information that way, so could we.

So, as students finish writing about one animal, they choose another and begin the process all over again. As I mentioned, some students work quickly, making their webs, finding appropriate information, and writing down that information on the templates. Others need more support. Therefore, by inviting students who work quickly to move on to new animal chapters, I allow them to work at their own pace. No child ends up hurrying or waiting for others to finish. It also gives students more opportunities to glean research tools and hone nonfiction writing skills.

One day, I have Eli share his work because he has completed one cycle of research and writing, and is about to embark on a second. Eli talks about not only the writing he did, but also his process of choosing an animal, making a web, finding information, and writing about his findings. In essence, Eli's share serves as my mini-lesson for the day, as he models his process for students who may not be quite as far along. Following his share, I speak to the class.

Benefits of Moving to Anthologies

- Builds confidence. In kindergarteners' and first graders' eyes, being able to handle chapter books is the epitome of being a good reader. Therefore, creating them makes students feel like competent writers.

- Allows students more independence because they are able to choose and write about a few animals that interest them, at their own pace.

- Eliminates the "I'm done" issue because there is not a clear "end" to the study. When students finish one animal, they begin another.

- Enables students to explore nonfiction text features. For example, when we are ready to publish, we organize our work according to a table of contents. Organizing a table of contents for more than one animal leads students toward a deeper level of understanding how nonfiction texts are organized.

Jodi: Eli has finished all of the templates on one animal and is ready to start working on a new one. What do you think Eli needs to do first when he starts on a new animal?

Fakoya: He needs to make a web.

Elijah: He has to write down all the things he knows already and then find out more.

Jodi: That's a great way to start. As you finish your first animal, we'll look at your work and make sure you have all of the information you can find. Then you may be ready to start working on another animal. Let's get to work.

This chapter demonstrated how the children and I turned research facts into writing—specifically, how we began using templates to create pages for individual animal books. During this process, sharing our research findings and writing strategies became integral to our work. In the next chapter, I look closely at what and how we shared.

Chapter 5

Sharing Our Information-Finding Process

F or students of any age, learning a new process is often over-whelming. Sharing strategies, working collaboratively, and airing frustrations often eases the transition into the new process. This reinforces that we are a team, working together. In this chapter, I show how I encourage students to share the process of finding information about animals.

Sharing Ideas in Whole-Class Meetings

After our first day of independent work, I can tell that some of the kids are feeling unsure of themselves. They are eager to write about animals, but because research is new to them, they struggle with gathering the information that informs that writing. So each day, after writing workshop, we share ideas. Here's an example of a typical exchange:

Jodi: How many of you felt like finding information was hard?

Class: (*Almost everyone raises his or her hand.*)

Jodi: Research is hard. It takes a lot of work and a lot of looking. Some days you may only be able to find a little bit of information. Some days you might find more information than you know what to do with. Each day will be different. The best thing for us to do is to share our ideas and strategies for finding information. That way, it will get easier for everyone. Did anyone do anything today that was helpful?

Donna: I found a book about horses.

Jodi: Where did you find it?

Donna: In the animal basket.

Jodi: So looking for books in our classroom library's animal basket is helpful.

As the study continues, I choose three or four children to share the work they've done, which usually relates to my mini-lesson for that day. I also may choose a student who is working through an issue. That way, as a class, we can suggest strategies to help that student.

At the beginning of the year, I model asking questions and making comments about the writing. Over time, as students begin to carry out their classmates' suggestions, they come to see themselves as "co-writing teachers" because their comments are often so useful. At first, students are inquisitive, sometimes in awe of what their classmates know about their animals. They might ask:

- *Why did you want to learn about that animal?*
- *Where did you get your information?*
- *How did you find that out?*

But as they begin to understand how to find information and apply it in writing, their comments become more focused on the writing itself:

- *I like the way you described where they live.*
- *I like the way you used details in your pictures.*
- *Do you know more about what they look like? Could you add that?*

In addition to post-workshop meetings, we take time to talk about our process at other parts of day, such as writing share and morning read-aloud. During a nonfiction study, our conversation about finding and sharing information is constant.

Sharing Resources in Writing Workshop

As we scour books for information, I encourage children to think beyond their own needs and help one another. For example, while looking for information on vultures, Declan and I come across some information on parrots, a topic that Bryan is researching. I urge Declan to show the information to Bryan. This "teamwork" mentality is essential to our success in writing nonfiction. Although students are working on independent projects, they come to see each other as members of a research team who they can turn to for ideas, strategies, and help.

Sharing this way boosts students' confidence and learning. And it often sets "animal book shuffle" into motion. Students find books and scour them first for their own purposes. If they can't find anything useful, they pass the book along to a classmate who might. If a group of students is working on the same animal, I encourage them to work alongside one another to provide support and inspiration, as this group researching turtles does:

Vinny:	How do turtles move?
Esmir:	Slowly.
Bryan:	Land turtles move slowly. Sea turtles can swim fast.
Vinny:	How do you know?
Bryan:	I wrote about turtles before.

Over time, students themselves can become even more valuable than the texts in our classroom.

Working Alongside Other Writers

At the start of the year, I assign students to heterogeneous groups for writing workshop. Unless problems arise, the groups stay together for the entire year, which allows members to get to know one another as writers, work collaboratively, and support one another. Storing student work and assessments in colored writing folders (i.e., red, green, yellow, blue, and purple) helps me manage the workshop.

However, during a nonfiction study, I sometimes suggest that students break from their groups and work next to a classmate who is writing about the same animal or who has already done research on that animal. That way, I foster interdependence without completely disrupting our writing workshop.

In this chapter, I explained methods of sharing information to foster independence during our nonfiction study. Having students acknowledge their problems and solve them together is a fundamental part of our writing workshop. In fact, the children become writing teachers of sorts. And the more they share ideas, strategies, and content with one another, the better their teaching becomes. In the next chapter, I explore the process of editing and compiling our books.

Chapter 6

Editing and Compiling Our Books

We're into week five of our nonfiction study. So far the students have picked topics, created webs, done research, filled in templates to create chapters, and shared their process. Now they are ready to compile their chapters into nonfiction anthologies.

Editing Our Books

Checking for Information

To prepare students for publishing, I start by having them check to make sure they've included all their web information in their templates. I introduce how this is done in a mini-lesson.

Jodi: We are almost finished with our animal books. Today you will be checking your chapters to make sure all of the information on your web is in your book. If it isn't, add it. If it is, work with a partner to check his or her work. Here are some things to keep in mind. (*Shows students a chart of these questions and reads them aloud.*):

> - *Did I add all of the details and information I know about this animal to my chapter?*
> - *Did I leave out any words?*
> - *Is what I'm writing true? Is it fact or opinion?*
> - *When I read my work aloud, how does it sound? Does it make sense?*
> - *Do my pictures accurately match my text?*

As the students work together, I confer with them and offer advice. I am surprised at how well they are able to help one another. For the most part, they welcome the ideas of their peers. Take Bryan and Justin, for example. Justin, who is writing about snakes, reads his work aloud: "Snakes have scales. They are slimy and slippery."

Bryan: Hey, you can't write that. That's your opinion.

Justin: But I think that they are slimy.

Bryan: You need to write only the facts. You can write other things you know about their skin.

Justin: They shed their skin.

Bryan: That's a fact. So you can add that.

When reviewing their work, students also need to ensure that their pictures match their text appropriately. If they don't, I ask students to revise the picture, revise the text, or add a caption that somehow links the text and the picture together. In the end, many don't end up changing text, but rather isolate missing words and add them, which is fine with me at this stage. The students feel empowered.

Checking for Spelling

During the drafting process, I don't focus on spelling. In my class, invented spelling is expected and accepted in initial stages of writing. I make sure, however, that students are spelling their animals' names correctly from the start, since they are using them frequently.

When preparing for publishing, I ask students to ask themselves:

> - *Are the names of my animals spelled correctly throughout my book?*
> - *Are all of the words from the word wall spelled correctly in my writing?*
> - *Are there words that I know aren't right, but don't know how to spell? If so, where can I look or who can I ask to find the correct spelling?*

I don't make my kindergarteners correct every word. For them, feeling successful as nonfiction writers is most important. For my first graders, I up the ante a bit. I encourage them to check words they should know and use resources to figure out the ones they don't.

Checking for Picture Details

Many students use pictures to share information, as well as words. So, while checking for written details, I check to make sure any pictures match the text.

I also ask students to make sure there's a picture on every page that they feel needs one. Some students draw their animals on each page. Others are more restrained. Some don't draw at all, using found images. For example, Eli, who is frustrated trying to depict his animal accurately, gets some information about the lion off of the Internet, which includes photos, and asks if he can use those photos instead of drawing images himself. Why not? I think. Photographs often accompany nonfiction texts. Eli cuts out the photographs and glues them onto pages in his book.

Using photographs allows Eli to work around his frustrations with drawing. He shares the idea with students who are experiencing similar problems.

Where a _LION_ lives

LIONS LIVE IN GRASS LANDS OF AFICA AND AUSTRLIA.

Eli's lion template with photographs

Compiling Our Books

Consolidating Chapters

The next step is to pull all of our writing together, in order. To get students started, I create a table-of-contents template that lists the headings on our individual pages and conduct a mini-lesson:

Jodi: We are almost ready to publish our books. We've checked our information, pictures, and writing. Now we need to get our pages in order so that it will be easy for our readers to find the information they're looking for. What are some ways you found information when you were reading through books?

Noah: Pictures.

Elijah: Index.

Esmir: On the computer.

Amanda: Table of contents.

Jodi: We used all of those things. We are going to create a table of contents for our books, which will help our readers go right to the information they need. I have a table-of-contents template for you to use. First, put your pages in the order they are on the table-of-contents template. (*Demonstrates organizing pages according to the template.*)

I give each student a photocopy of the template. Usually, students spend the entire writing workshop putting their pages in order and helping classmates. When they're finished, they paperclip the pages together. (See Appendix C for a reproducible template.)

Table of Contents

Chapter		Page
What a	looks like	
What a	eats	
How a	moves	
How a	grows	
Where a	lives	
How a	protects itself	
How a	takes care of its babies	

Writing a Table of Contents

Once our pages are in order, we add page numbers to them and to the table of contents. I demonstrate how to do this on my monkey book.

Jodi: Today you are going to number your pages and then add those page numbers to your table of contents. The first thing you will do is write the chapter title on the table-of-contents page, where it says, "Chapter ___." (*Writes "Monkeys" in the space.*) Then, I'll move on to the page numbers. In my monkey book, I'm going to write the number one in the corner of the "What a

Monkey Looks Like" page. (*Numbers the page.*) And then, on my table-of-contents page, I'm going to write the number one next to where it says "What a Monkey Looks Like." (*Applies the page number to the table of contents.*) Then I'll go to page two and do the same thing. When you finish one animal, I'll give you a new table-of-contents page so that you can start working on Chapter 2. I'll help you when you get there.

Filling in the table of contents for their first chapter is not a problem. Almost every child can order and number their pages accurately. At this point in the study, students are so familiar with the headings, that even my emergent readers are comfortable with the amount of reading necessary to accomplish the task.

The second and third chapters, however, are more challenging because the page numbers continue from the first chapter. I wind up helping many children with this task, using time outside of writing workshop to confer individually with them.

Creating Chapter Dividers and Endpapers

Creating chapter dividers and endpapers elevate the work from a piece of writing to a published piece of work. It also gives students a sense of accomplishment.

I introduce these elements with a favorite read-aloud book: *Owl Babies* by Martin Waddell. Besides being a wonderful tale about an owl and her chicks, the book has beautiful endpapers that resemble an owl's wing feathers. I show students the endpapers from *Owl*

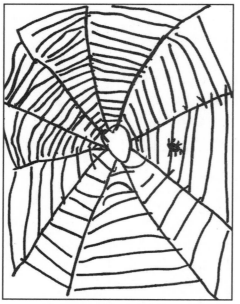

One of Cosmo's chapters is about spiders. So he uses a spider web as one of his book endpapers.

Noah writes about crabs in one of his chapters. So on his chapter divider, he drew a crab.

Alicia's book includes chapters about butterflies and tigers. So she includes details inspired by both animals on her endpapers, close-ups of a butterfly wing and a tiger stripe.

Babies and we talk about how the illustrator uses one close-up part of the animal rather than the whole animal.

The students decide to apply the illustrator's idea to their own books. For the chapter dividers, they suggest using a detail that gives a hint of the animal, such as stripes, spots, or paw prints. For the endpapers, they suggest using a combination of details inspired by all of the animals described in the anthology.

I have students use 8½" x 11" poster-board for endpapers and chapter dividers, which creates a finished look and provides extra reinforcement.

Favorite Picture Books for an Animal Study

A Pinky Is a Baby Mouse: And Other Baby Animal Names by Pam Muñoz Ryan (Hyperion)

Does a Kangaroo Have a Mother, Too? by Eric Carle (HarperCollins)

Verdi by Janell Cannon (Harcourt)

Owl Babies by Martin Waddell (Candlewick Press)

Writing an "About the Researcher" Page

When our chapters are compiled, tables of contents filled out, and chapter dividers and endpapers assembled, we are ready to work on our "about the researcher" page.

Often, when I read books aloud, I share the "about the author" page with students, which gives them a sense of the writer's background and, perhaps, insight into his or her inspiration for the story. So, when the time came to publish our books, it seemed only natural for students to include a similar page about themselves. Rather than calling it "about the author," though, I renamed it "about the researcher," because it suggested all the fastidious, fact-finding work that went into the book.

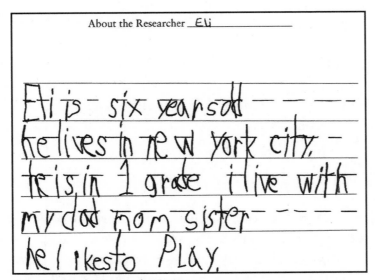

About the Researcher Eli

Eli is six years old
he lives in new york city.
he is in 1 grade i live with
my dad mom sister
he likes to play.

Eli's "About the Researcher" page

As a class, we share ideas for information to include. Students draft their blurbs, mentioning their ages, locations, and favorite pastimes. (See Appendix D for a reproducible template.)

Titling Our Books

Students are free to choose whatever title seems appropriate. Noah simply called his book *Noah's Animal Book*. Often they use published works to guide them. Amanda chose *All About Frogs and Cats and Chickens and Owls*. Eli chose *Animal Geographics*.

Binding Our Books

Since students' books contain tables of contents, chapter dividers, endpapers, and as many as four chapters, the final product can be long—up to 30 pages. So securing pages well is important. For our covers, we use oak-tag paper. For our bindings, we use sturdy metal rings, similar to loose-leaf binder rings, which are wonderful for binding thick documents. To prevent ripping, we put reinforcements on all of our pages before binding them together.

After their books are bound, students desperately want to share the information they gathered. After all, that's what experts do—they share their knowledge. So we have a publishing party for our families and other classes. (See Chapter 9 for details.)

Creating a Class Treasury of Animals

In addition to creating individual chapter books (which eventually go home), we put together a class animal anthology (which remains in the classroom). This anthology is a collection of *all* of the chapters the students write for their individual books.

After students complete their books, I make copies of their pages. Then, as a class, we organize alphabetically all the animals and assemble the chapters, adding chapter dividers and endpapers. This compilation becomes a class treasury of our animal knowledge.

In this chapter, I focused on moving our work from writing single pages to a connected piece. The students researched and wrote diligently to compile books of their own. In the next chapter, I show how the children work together to create a whole-class book based on an inquiry question.

Chapter 7

Extending Our Study

O ur study takes on many dimensions and leads us in many directions beyond writing. Animals often become the subject of the songs we sing, the poems and books we read, and the art we create. In this chapter, I discuss a whole-class extension of our individual projects.

Each morning during our study, I choose an animal book to read aloud. One morning I read Eric Carle's *Does a Kangaroo Have a Mother, Too?* which explores the various names for animal mothers, fathers, babies, and groups (for example, a mother deer is a doe, a father is a buck, a baby is a fawn, and a group is a herd). My class is intrigued by all the interesting names. We begin wondering about animals not listed in Eric Carle's book, and a whole-class research project is born.

Whole-Class Research on Animal Names

Since the students are already working on individual books, I decide that, together, we will compile a whole-class book about animal mothers, fathers, and babies.

The following morning, we make a chart based on information from the Eric Carle book:

Animal	Mother	Father	Baby	Group
Kangaroo	Flyer	Boomer	Joey	Troop, Mob, or Herd
Lion	Lioness	Lion	Cub	Pride
Giraffe	Cow	Bull	Calf	Tower or Herd
Penguin	Dam	Sire	Chick	Colony or Parade
Swan	Pen	Cob	Cygnet	Wedge or Herd
Fox	Vixen	Dog Fox	Cub or Pup	Pack or Skulk
Dolphin	Cow	Bull	Calf	School or Pod
Sheep	Ewe	Ram	Lamb	Flock
Bear	Sow	Boar	Cub	Pack or Sloth
Elephant	Cow	Bull	Calf	Herd
Monkey	Mother	Father	Infant	Group, Troop, or Tribe
Deer	Doe	Buck	Fawn	Herd

After we fill in all the information from the book, I ask the students for other kinds of animals to add to the chart. Then I encourage them to look up information on those animals or keep an eye out for it as they do research for their independent projects. As they find facts, they add them to our class chart.

In the first few days of the project, we find some names. However, that success starts to wane after a few days. So, once again, I enlist the help of families. I send home a note requesting that each child, if possible, find information on a specific animal that I assign.

During our morning meeting, we add our newly acquired facts to our growing chart of animal names. One family even finds a Web site that contains just the information we need. We are so excited.

As our chart grows, we begin to see connections. For example,

Homework   ∿OAH

For our research on animals, our class is writing a book about what mother, father, baby, and groups of animals are called.

Please help your child find out the following information for a: Duck

A **mother** is called a

DUCK

A **father** is called a

dRAKE

A **baby** is called a

DUCKLiNG

A **group** is called a

bRACE Team

Homework on animal names

the name of a baby cow is a calf. The name of a baby dolphin is also a calf and both of their mothers are called cows. These similarities fascinate students and they begin to look for them in their research.

Web Sites for Animal Facts

Animal Group Names:
http://www.stalking.co.uk/group.html

Animal Kingdom, animal names page:
http://www.teach-at-home.com/fastfacts/animalkingdom/Names.asp

Fact Monster, animal science page:
http://www.factmonster.com/ipka/A0872847.html

Fairfax County, Virginia, animal page:
http://www.co.fairfax.va.us/library/Faq/animal.htm

Names of Males, Females, Babies, and Groups:
http://www.enchantedlearning.com/subjects/animals/Animalbabies.shtml

Formatting Our Whole-Class Book

Once we have gathered all of our research on animal names, we need to figure out a format for the class book. Inspired by Carle's book, students decide to address one animal per page. I map out two layout options, using alternating colors to highlight the information, and put them up for a vote. The class chooses option 2. The following day, during work centers, we begin working.

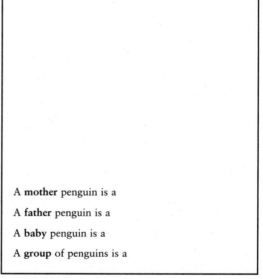

A **mother** penguin is called a	A **father** penguin is called a
A **baby** penguin is called a	A **group** of penguins is called a

Book format, option 1

A **mother** penguin is a

A **father** penguin is a

A **baby** penguin is a

A **group** of penguins is a

Book format, option 2

Page from the finished book

Each student picks an animal from the chart. Then using the phrase, "A _____ (animal) is a _____," he or she inserts the correct information, with words and pictures, and creates a page. The result is a big book of animal names that the children would continue to read for the rest of the year. They could take pride in the fact that each of them wrote and/or illustrated at least one of the pages.

A Sticky Situation

Without even thinking about the consequences, I had given Emma "dog" to research. One morning her mom came in, concerned because the formal name for a female dog is "bitch." She wasn't sure how to proceed with Emma—and neither was I. From the Web-site list, I noticed that any female dog relative (wolves, etc.) is called "bitch." I was tempted to not even address it with the class. However, we were including ferrets and turtles and kangaroos. How could we exclude the favored dog?! At this point, my students were well aware that this was a nonfiction study—that we were researchers looking for facts. I hoped that this would lay the foundation for a serious conversation.

During one morning meeting, while adding to our chart, I discussed Emma's research with the class. "The name of a female dog is a name you may or may not have heard being used very differently," I said, taking a deep breath. "It's a name that is sometimes used as a curse word. I wasn't going to include it in our research, but I think you can handle it. Emma and I would like to share her information with you, knowing that when this word is used in the classroom it will be used appropriately."

After talking about the term "bitch," and its acceptable use, the children were fine and so were their families. With a solid understanding of the term, the students were able to use it like researchers when addressing a mother wolf, fox, and other animals like them. I expected that the children would be fine, and they were.

In this chapter, we took a turn from our independent projects to a class project on animal names. We looked at compiling research to make one book together. In the following chapter, I discuss other ways I enhance our nonfiction study.

Chapter 8

Promoting Nonfiction Writing Throughout the Day

onfiction writing is woven into many other components of my curriculum, beyond writing workshop. In fact, it permeates the day. In this chapter, I look at how music, art, and literature help to expose my students to factual information in an informal, accessible manner. During our animal study, I use music, art, and literature to focus on animal habitats, extinction, and family life, which builds upon the foundation students are forming in their own research.

Songs

Each morning, I put a familiar song on our CD player as a cue for the students to come join me on the rug. Once gathered, I introduce them to a new song. We listen to it once or twice and talk a little about the lyrics. I place the lyrics of new songs in a special folder for each student. These folders provide excellent material for a shared reading or partner reading.

We also listen to music after recess and lunch to help us relax and refocus. We sing three songs after lunch, old and new songs chosen by the "kid of the day."

Kid of the Day

The kid of the day has many responsibilities such as line leader and door hold, attendance taker, and picker of after-lunch songs. I rotate the kid of the day daily and post a list so that students know when their turn is coming up.

For every kind of study, there are songs to complement it. These songs bolster understanding of the topic under investigation. Children gain an incredible amount of information from the lyrics—information that often becomes part of their research. Here are some of the songs we sang during our animal unit:

Tom Chapin:
  "Two Kinds of Seagulls"

John McCutcheon:
  "All God's Critters"
  "Rubber Blubber Whale"

Sarah Weeks:
  "I'm an Animal"
  "Pretty Tree"
  "Being Extinct"
  "Take It Slow"
  "Pad, Pad, Pad"
  "Crocodile Smile"
  "Don't Discover Me"
  "Piece of the Jungle"

Poems

Poetry adds dimension to our study, too. Every week, I choose a Poem of the Week that relates to animals. Some poems contain beautiful language and imagery. Some are informational, others are silly, and others are a little bit of both.

There are many books available with poems about animals. One of my favorites is *Animal Trunk* by Charles Ghigna, which contains poems that are factual and funny. Most students can read and understand them easily. I encourage my students to use facts from these poems in their research. Poetry is another genre through which children can learn about any topic.

> ### Favorite Poetry Books for an Animal Study
>
> *Animal Trunk: Silly Poems to Read Aloud* by Charles Ghigna (Harry N. Abrams)
>
> *The Beauty of the Beast: Poems from the Animal Kingdom* by Jack Prelutsky (Knopf)
>
> *Just Us Two: Poems About Animal Dads* by Joyce Sidman (Millbrook Press)

Read Alouds

Every day, I read a nonfiction or fiction animal book to the class to support our study. With a nonfiction book, we discuss the text features such as captions and indexes. We look at complex vocabulary and explore strategies for understanding it. My students never seem to tire of the facts and photographs in the books. Those elements always draw them in.

With a fiction book, we try to separate myth and reality. I ask questions such as, "Which parts do you think are true?" "Which parts aren't?" "What can we learn about this animal from this book?" "Does this information match the information we already have?" "Does it make sense to us based on what we know?"

Our read-aloud conversations allow us to apply knowledge we have gathered and put it to the test. Students are always delighted to see that fiction books incorporate nonfiction elements.

Poem of the Week

I choose a poem of the week and write it on chart paper for all to see. Each day during the week, the poem is used for various purposes.

Monday, we read the poem three times together.

Tuesday, we read the poem together once and then begin to find "word wall words," or words we know.

Wednesday, we read the poem once together before finding more familiar words, perhaps more word wall words, or other words that are common but not yet on our word wall. We also look for words that we may want to add to our word wall. For example, when we were studying water in our class science study we decided that "water" and "rain" were two words that we wanted to add to our word wall, since we would be using them frequently in our discussions and in our writing. After finding these words we once again re-read the poem chorally, with me reading the non-underlined text and the students reading the words they now know.

Thursday, we look for more challenge words (words that may be specific to the poem, but not in our common realm of knowledge—potato, glasses, and so forth), rhymes, or a pattern in the poem.

Friday, we read the poem once together and then the children read it aloud as a class to me.

—from *Joyful Ways to Teach Young Children to Write Poetry* by Jodi Weisbart (Scholastic)

Read alouds also give students an opportunity to see how professional writers present what they know. By studying texts closely, students gain an understanding of titles, subheadings, and sequence. As they make connections between read-aloud texts and their own writing, their work improves.

Games

One of the games we love to play is "1-2-3 What Do You See?" It allows the students to be creative, move around, and make connections to the unit of study by acting, literally, like animals. I start by having the children stand up and prepare themselves to move around. Then I announce, "1-2-3..."

Class:	What do you see?
Jodi:	I see a monkey in front of me.
Class:	(*Acts like monkeys.*)
Jodi:	1-2-3...
Class:	(*Freezes.*) What do you see?
Jodi:	I see an elephant in front of me.
Class:	(*Acts like elephants.*)

As the children become comfortable with the game, I ask them to take the lead:

Liana:	1-2-3 . . .
Class:	What do you see?
Liana:	I see a ferret in front of me.

Some students know what ferrets look like and how they move. Others aren't quite sure. Sharing of knowledge informally gives students a way to access new information, without needing to research it.

"1-2-3 What Do You See?" works for any unit of study. During a study on community, for example, our subjects moved from frogs and turtles to bus drivers and pizza makers. You can play it for two minutes or twenty minutes. It is especially effective as a transition activity.

Field Trips

Our study moves beyond our classroom. With clipboards in hand, we go to the Staten Island Zoo, Central Park Zoo, Bronx Zoo, and Alley Pond Environmental Center. We participate in guided programs on animals and animal classification. We learn the difference between mammals and reptiles. We ask the zoologists questions about taking care of the animals. This kind of hands-on research takes our study to another level. No longer are we merely reading about the animals, we are observing them—and becoming animal experts in the process.

Beforehand, we prepare interview questions to ask during the trip. When we arrive, we shoot photographs, draw pictures, and take notes, and use the material we gather to support our research and writing.

Field trips give students a sense of purpose and direction. Students know they are on the trip to gather information and will be responsible for sharing new knowledge in some manner later. This expectation elevates the experience from an enjoyable day at the zoo to a learning adventure.

Art Projects

As our research continues, our animals became almost real to us—so much so that I ask students to make three-dimensional representations of them. In collaboration with the art teacher and many parent volunteers, we create a papier-mâché zoo.

The art teacher has the children make detailed drawings of their animals from photographs, encouraging them to focus on special features such as beaks and claws. At the same time, I ask students to collect boxes of all shapes and sizes, tubes, and containers, and invite parents to help us make our constructions.

Dear Families,

We'd like to do a papier mâché animal project. We need your help.

1) Talk to your child about which animal he/she would like to make based on the ones he/she has been writing about.

2) Send in:
small boxes (like spaghetti, pasta)
balloons
newspaper (LOTS!)
masking tape (LOTS!)
cereal boxes
toilet paper rolls (LOTS!)
paper towel rolls (LOTS!)

Send in for the week of 22nd

3) Would you like to help?

We'll have 1 day of assembling the structures
1 day of papier mâché
1 day of painting
Let us know!

Look for sign up sheet soon

Letter to families

Students work in small groups, making frames for their animals out of cardboard boxes, cardboard tubes, and balloons that parents contribute, using tape to fasten everything together. The following day, I set out newspaper and flour-and-water paste, and students coat their frames with slimy strips. We are messy, but productive. Our structures dry over the next few days.

The following week, students paint their structures. They add color, texture, and facial features that make the animals come alive. When they finish, I hang the animals from the lights. Our classroom is immediately transformed into a magical, fantastical zoo.

When the students see their animals hanging up for the first time, their jaws drop. They can't believe all of the creatures dangling above their heads. They're proud of their work. And because they worked so closely during the research process, they not only became experts on their own animals, but on everyone else's as well. Liana can tell me all about her ferret as well as Esmir's turtle. Eli could rattle off facts about his prairie dog *and* Cosmo's tiger. Their artwork was the finishing touch to a multi-dimensional nonfiction study.

Chapter 9

Celebrating What We've Learned

In my classroom, I live by the motto: "Work hard and celebrate often." I expect my students to work hard and they do. And they love to celebrate. But at celebrations, we do more than enjoy ourselves. We share our knowledge.

At the end of the nonfiction study, we have a publishing party. We send invitations to families and other teachers. Each student chooses a chapter from his or her book to read aloud at the party, and practices beforehand in front of other classes.

At the start of the party, we sing an animal song from our collection, "Two Kinds of Seagulls." Guests wander around the room marveling at our animal sculptures hanging from the ceiling. Then the student-researchers read aloud their work to them. From there, I ask families to browse through all the books, encouraging them to take time to read the "About the Researcher" pages and notice the endpapers, chapter dividers, and tables of contents. I want them to fully appreciate the amount of work their children accomplished. And I want them to celebrate that work.

During the rest of the year, I notice students gravitating toward their own books more than toward others. Our class book on animal names becomes a class favorite. In fact, I often catch students and grown-ups reading it together in the first few minutes of the morning. It is clear that students feel ownership of this book and the information they gathered to create it.

Closing Thoughts

As writing teachers, we want to inspire our students, expose them to a variety of genres, and build their confidence so that they view themselves as writers. From an early age, children understand and can tell stories orally. When they enter school, or perhaps before, they begin to understand that pictures and words can also tell stories. Our students have barrels of untapped stories waiting to be released. They are experts on many, many things—most particularly, on their own lives.

I hope that, by studying nonfiction writing, students will discover new areas of expertise and interest. In the early grades it's important to use what students know as the foundation for learning. Building on that knowledge sets the stage for a successful year of writing nonfiction.

Topics for Mini-Lessons
That Boost Nonfiction Writing

- Distinguishing fiction and nonfiction

- Planning with a web

- Revisiting a web

- Using the index

- Using the table of contents

- Distinguishing fact and opinion

- Using a web to inform your writing

- Using print resources to gather information

- Writing captions for illustrations and photos

- Introducing reading strategies for nonfiction

- Creating chapter dividers and endpapers

- Writing "About the Researcher" pages

See page 46 for an explanation of how to use this reproducible.

Table of Contents

Chapter	Page
What a _____ looks like	_____
What a _____ eats	_____
How a _____ moves	_____
How a _____ grows	_____
Where a _____ lives	_____
How a _____ protects itself	_____
How a _____ takes care of its babies	_____
_____	_____
_____	_____
_____	_____

See page 58 for an explanation of how to use this reproducible.

About the Researcher

_____

See page 62 for an explanation of how to use this reproducible.

Scholastic Professional Books   Introducing Nonfiction Writing in the Early Grades   Appendix D